John A. Symonds

Michael Angelo Buonarroti

his sonnets now for the first time translated into rhymed English

John A. Symonds

Michael Angelo Buonarroti
his sonnets now for the first time translated into rhymed English

ISBN/EAN: 9783337266059

Printed in Europe, USA, Canada, Australia, Japan

Cover: Foto ©Thomas Meinert / pixelio.de

More available books at **www.hansebooks.com**

ह

THE SONNETS

OF

MICHAEL ANGELO BUONARROTI

THOU 'RT dead of dying, and art made divine;
     Nor need'st thou fear to change or life or will;
     Wherefore my soul well-nigh doth envy thine.
Fortune and time across thy threshold still
     Shall dare not pass, the which mid us below
     Bring doubtful joyance blent with certain ill.
Clouds are there none to dim for thee heaven's glow;
     The measured hours compel not thee at all;
     Chance or necessity thou canst not know.
Thy splendour wanes not when our night doth fall,
     Nor waxes with day's light however clear,
     Nor when our suns the season's warmth recall.

MICHAEL ANGELO:

On His Father's Death.

VITTORIA COLONNA
From a Design by Michael Angelo

MICHAEL ANGELO
BUONARROTI

His Sonnets

Now for the first time translated into
rhymed English by

John Addington Symonds.

Printed for Thomas B. Mosher
and Published by him at
37 Exchange Street, Portland,
Maine. MdcccXcv.

CONTENTS.

									PAGE.
PROEM,	.	.	.	.	.	.	.		8
SONNETS,	.		.	.	.	.	.		11
NOTES,	.	.	.	.	.	.	.	.	99
APPENDICES,	.	.	.	.	.	.			107

PROEM.

THE PHILOSOPHIC FLIGHT.

Poi che spiegate.

Now *that these wings to speed my wish ascend,*
The more I feel vast air beneath my feet,
The more toward boundless air on pinions fleet,
Spurning the earth, soaring to heaven, I tend:
Nor makes them stoop their flight the direful end
Of Dædal's son; but upward still they beat:—
What life the while with my life can compete,
Though dead to earth at last I shall descend?
My own heart's voice in the void air I hear:
Where wilt thou bear me, O rash man? Recall
Thy daring will! This boldness waits on fear!
Dread not, I answer, that tremendous fall:
Strike through the clouds, and smile when death is
near,
If death so glorious be our doom at all!

THE SONNETS

OF

MICHAEL ANGELO BUONARROTI

Mr. Symonds originally printed his version of The Sonnets of Michael Angelo in connexion with those of Tommaso Campanella, (8vo, London, 1878,) and placed a Greek motto on the title-page:

Χρύσεων χάλκεια

The introduction to this edition having become superseded to a large extent by his later and more adequate handling of the subject, is not here included. The reader who desires to study the freshest presentation of the Sonnets, would therefore do well to consult *Symonds' Life of Michelangelo Buonarroti*, (2 vols. 8vo, London, 1893.)

Advantage has been had of the *Life* to collect and include in *The Bibelot Edition*, those textual revisions in the translation scattered through its pages: changes that had Mr. Symonds lived, he would no doubt, himself, put forth in due season.

I.

ON DANTE ALIGHIERI.

Dal ciel discese.

FROM *heaven his spirit came, and robed in clay,*
  The realms of justice and of mercy trod:
  Then rose a living man to gaze on God,
  That he might make the truth as clear as day.
For that pure star, that brightened with his ray
  The undeserving nest where I was born,
  The whole wide world would be a prize to scorn;
  None but his Maker can due guerdon pay.
I speak of Dante, whose high work remains
  Unknown, unhonoured by that thankless brood,
  Who only to just men deny their wage.
Were I but he! Born for like lingering pains,
  Against his exile coupled with his good
  I'd gladly change the world's best heritage!

II.

ON DANTE ALIGHIERI.

Quante dirne si de'.

No tongue can tell of him what should be told,
  For on blind eyes his splendour shines too strong;
  'Twere easier to blame those who wrought him wrong,
  Than sound his least praise with a mouth of gold.
He to explore the place of pain was bold,
  Then soared to God, to teach our souls by song;
  The gates heaven oped to bear his feet along,
  Against his just desire his country rolled.
Thankless I call her, and to her own pain
  The nurse of fell mischance; for sign take this,
  That ever to the best she deals more scorn:
Among a thousand proofs let one remain;
  Though ne'er was fortune more unjust than his,
  His equal or his better ne'er was born.

III.

TO POPE JULIUS II.

Signor, se vero è.

My Lord! if ever ancient saw spake sooth,
    Hear this which saith: *Who can, doth never will.*
    Lo! thou hast lent thine ear to fables still,
    Rewarding those who hate the name of truth.
I am thy **drudge** and have been from my youth —
    Thine, like the rays which the sun's circle fill;
    Yet of my dear time's waste thou **think'st** no ill:
    The more I toil, the less I move thy ruth.
Once 'twas my hope to raise me by thy height;
    But 'tis the balance and the powerful sword
    Of Justice, not false Echo, that we need.
Heaven, as it seems, plants virtue in despite
    Here on the earth, if this be our reward —
    To seek for fruit on trees too dry to breed.

xiii

IV.

ON ROME IN THE PONTIFICATE OF JULIUS II.

Qua si fa elmi.

HERE *helms and swords are made of chalices:*
The blood of Christ is sold so much the quart:
His cross and thorns are spears and shields; and
  short
Must be the time ere even His patience cease.
Nay let Him come no more to raise the fees
Of this foul sacrilege beyond report!
For Rome still flays and sells Him at the court,
Where paths are closed to virtue's fair increase.
Now were fit time for me to scrape a treasure!
Seeing that work and gain are gone; while he
Who wears the robe, is my Medusa still.
God welcomes poverty perchance with pleasure:
But of that better life what hope have we,
When the blessed banner leads to nought but ill?

V.

ON THE PAINTING OF THE SISTINE CHAPEL.

TO GIOVANNI DA PISTOJA.

I' ho già fatto un gozzo.

I 'VE *grown a goitre by dwelling in this den —*
    As cats from stagnant streams in Lombardy,
    Or in what other land they hap to be —
    Which drives the belly close beneath the chin :
My beard turns up to heaven ; my nape falls in,
    Fixed on my spine : my breast-bone visibly
    Grows like a harp : a rich embroidery
    Bedews my face from brush-drops thick and thin.
My loins into my paunch like levers grind :
    My buttock like a crupper bears my weight ;
    My feet unguided wander to and fro ;
In front my skin grows loose and long ; behind,
    By bending it becomes more taut and strait ;
    Crosswise I strain me like a Syrian bow :
        Whence false and quaint, I know,
    Must be the fruit of squinting brain and eye ;
    For ill can aim the gun that bends awry.
        Come then, Giovanni, try
    To succour my dead pictures and my fame ;
    Since foul I fare and painting is my shame.

xv

VI.

INVECTIVE AGAINST THE PEOPLE OF PISTOJA.

I' l' ho, vostra mercè.

I'VE gotten it, thanks to your courtesy,
  And I have read it twenty times or so :
    Thus much may your sharp snarling profit you,
    As food our flesh filled to satiety.
After I left you, I could plainly see
    How Cain was of your ancestors : I know
    You do not shame his lineage, for lo,
    Your brother's good still seems your injury.
Envious you are, and proud, and foes to heaven ;
    Love of your neighbour still you loathe and hate, .
    And only seek what must your ruin be.
If to 'Pistoja Dante's curse was given,
    Bear that in mind! Enough! 'But if you prate
    Praises of Florence, 'tis to wheedle me.
                    A priceless jewel she :
    Doubtless : but this you cannot understand :
    For pigmy virtue grasps not aught so grand.

xvi

VII.

TO LUIGI DEL RICCIO.

Nel dolce d' una.

I T *happens that the sweet unfathomed sea*
  Of seeming courtesy sometimes doth hide
    Offence to life and honour.   This descried,
    I hold less dear the health restored to me.
He who lends wings of hope, while secretly
    He spreads a traitorous snare by the wayside,
    Hath dulled the flame of love, and mortified
    Friendship where friendship burns most fervently.
Keep then, my dear Luigi, clear and pure,
    That ancient love to which my life I owe,
    That neither wind nor storm its calm may mar.
For wrath and pain our gratitude obscure;
    And if the truest truth of love I know,
    One pang outweighs a thousand pleasures far.

VIII.

AFTER THE DEATH OF CECCHINO BRACCI.

TO LUIGI DEL RICCIO.

A pena prima.

S CARCE *had I seen for the first time his eyes,*
  Which to your living eyes were life and light,
  When, closed at last in death's injurious night,
  He opened them on God in Paradise.
I know it and I weep,—too late made wise:
  Yet was the fault not mine; for death's fell spite
  Robbed my desire of that supreme delight
  Which in your better memory never dies.
Therefore, Luigi, if the task be mine
  To make unique Cecchino smile in stone
  For ever, now that earth hath made him dim,
If the beloved within the lover shine,
  Since art without him cannot work alone,
  You must I carve to tell the world of him.

IX.

THANKS FOR A GIFT.

Al zucchero, alla mula.

THE sugar, candles, and the saddled mule,
  Together with your cask of malvoisie,
  So far exceed all my necessity
  That Michael and not I my debt must rule.
In such a glassy calm the breezes fool
  My sinking sails, so that amid the sea
  My bark hath missed her way, and seems to be
  A wisp of straw whirled on a weltering pool.
To yield thee gift for gift and grace for grace,
  For food and drink and carriage to and fro,
  For all my need in every time and place,
O my dear Lord, matched with the much I owe,
  All that I am were no real recompense:
  Paying a debt is not munificence.

X.

ON HIS MISTRESS FAUSTINA MANCINA.

TO GANDOLFO PORRINO.

La nuova alta beltà.

THAT *new transcendent fair who seems to be*
Peerless in heaven as in this world of woe,
(The common folk, too blind her worth to know
And worship, called her Left Arm wantonly),
Was made, full well I know, for only thee :
Nor could I carve or paint the glorious show
Of that fair face : to life thou needs must go,
To gain the favor thou dost crave of me.
If like the sun each star of heaven outshining,
She conquers and outsoars our soaring thought,
This bids thee rate her worth at its real price.
Therefore to satisfy thy ceaseless pining,
Once more in heaven hath God her beauty wrought :
God and not I can people Paradise.

XI.

ON THE LIVES OF THE PAINTERS.

TO GIORGIO VASARI.

Se con lo stile.

WITH *pencil and with palette hitherto*
  You made your art high Nature's paragon;
  Nay more, from Nature her own prize you won,
  Making what she made fair more fair to view.
Now that your learnéd hand with labour new
  Of pen and ink a worthier work hath done,
  What erst you lacked, what still remained her own,
  The power of giving life, is gained for you.
If men in any age with Nature vied
  In beauteous workmanship, they had to yield
  When to the fated end years brought their name.
You, re-illuming memories that died,
  In spite of Time and Nature have revealed
  For them and for yourself eternal fame.

XII.

A MATCHLESS COURTESY.

TO VITTORIA COLONNA.

Felice spirto.

BLEST *spirit, who with loving tenderness*
    Quickenest my heart, so old and near to die,
    Who 'mid thy joys on me dost bend an eye
    Though many nobler men around thee press!
As thou wert erewhile wont my sight to bless,
    So to console my mind thou now dost fly;
    Hope therefore stills the pangs of memory,
    Which, coupled with desire, my soul distress.
So finding in thee grace to plead for me—
    Thy thoughts for me sunk in so sad a case—
    He who now writes returns thee thanks for these.
Lo! it were foul and monstrous usury
    To send thee ugliest paintings in the place
    Of thy fair spirit's living phantasies.

.

XIII.

BRAZEN GIFTS FOR GOLDEN.

TO VITTORIA COLONNA.

Per esser manco almen.

Seeking at least to be not all unfit
    For thy sublime and boundless courtesy,
    My lowly thoughts at first were fain to try
    What they could yield for grace so infinite.
But now I know my unassisted wit
    Is all too weak to make me soar so high ;
    For pardon, lady, for this fault I cry,
    And wiser still I grow remembering it.
Yea, well I see what folly 'twere to think
    That largess dropped from thee like dews from
        heaven
    Could e'er be paid by work so frail as mine !
To nothingness my art and talent sink ;
    He fails who from his mortal stores hath given
    A thousandfold to match one gift divine.

XIV.

THE MODEL AND THE STATUE.

TO VITTORIA COLONNA.

Da che concetto.

WHEN *divine Art conceives a form and face,*
She bids the craftsman for his first essay
To shape a simple model in mere clay:
This is the earliest birth of Art's embrace.
From the live marble in the second place
His mallet brings into the light of day
A thing so beautiful that who can say
When time shall conquer that immortal grace?
Thus my own model I was born to be —
The model of that nobler self, whereto
Schooled by your pity, lady, I shall grow.
Each overplus and each deficiency
You will make good. What penance then is due
For my fierce heat, chastened and taught by you?

XIV.

THE MODEL AND THE STATUE.

TO VITTORIA COLONNA.

Se ben concetto.

WHEN *that which is divine in us doth try*
To shape a face, both brain and hand unite
To give, from a mere model frail and slight,
Life to the stone by Art's free energy.
Thus too before the painter dares to ply
Paint-brush or canvas, he is wont to write
Sketches on scraps of paper, and invite
Wise minds to judge his figured history.
So, born a model rude and mean to be
Of my poor self, I gain a nobler birth,
Lady, from you, you fountain of all worth!
Each overplus and each deficiency
You will make good.   What penance then is due
For my fierce heat, chastened and taught by you?

THE LOVER AND THE SCULPTOR.

Non ha l' ottimo artista.

THE best of artists hath no thought to show
   Which the rough stone in its superfluous shell
   Doth not include: to break the marble spell
Is all the hand that serves the brain can do.
The ill I shun, the good I seek, even so
   In thee, fair lady, proud, ineffable,
   Lies hidden: but the art I wield so well
Works adverse to my wish, and lays me low.
Therefore not love, nor thy transcendent face,
   Nor cruelty, nor fortune, nor disdain,
   Cause my mischance, nor fate, nor destiny;
Since in thy heart thou carriest death and grace
   Enclosed together, and my worthless brain
   Can draw forth only death to feed on me.

LOVE AND ART.

Sì come nella penna.

A s *pen and ink alike serve him who sings*
  In high or low or intermediate style;
  As the same stone hath shapes both rich and vile
  To match the fancies that each master brings;
So, my loved lord, within thy bosom springs
  Pride mixed with meekness and kind thoughts that
    smile:
  Whence I draw nought, my sad self to beguile,
  But what my face shows — dark imaginings.
He who for seed sows sorrow, tears, and sighs,
  (The dews that fall from heaven, though pure and
    clear,
  From different germs take divers qualities)
Must needs reap grief and garner weeping eyes;
  And he who looks on beauty with sad cheer,
  Gains doubtful hope and certain miseries.

THE ARTIST AND HIS WORK.

Com' esser, donna, può.

How can that be, lady, which all men learn
  By long experience? Shapes that seem alive,
  Wrought in hard mountain marble, will survive
  Their maker, whom the years to dust return!
Thus to effect cause yields. Art hath her turn,
  And triumphs over Nature. I, who strive
  With Sculpture, know this well; her wonders live
  In spite of time and death, those tyrants stern.
So I can give long life to both of us
  In either way, by colour or by stone,
  Making the semblance of thy face and mine.
Centuries hence when both are buried, thus
  Thy beauty and my sadness shall be shown,
  And men shall say, ' For her 'twas wise to pine.'

XVIII.

BEAUTY AND THE ARTIST.

Al cor di zolfo.

A HEART of flaming sulphur, flesh of tow,
    'Bones of dry wood, a soul without a guide
    To curb the fiery will, the ruffling pride
    Of fierce desires that from the passions flow ;
A sightless mind that weak and lame doth go
    Mid snares and pitfals scattered far and wide ; —
    What wonder if the first chance brand applied
    To fuel massed like this should make it glow ?
Add beauteous art, which, brought with us from heaven,
    Will conquer nature ; — so divine a power
    Belongs to him who strives with every nerve.
If I was made for art, from childhood given
    A 'prey for burning beauty to devour,
    I blame the mistress I was born to serve.

THE AMULET OF LOVE.

Io mi son caro assai più.

FAR more than I was wont myself I prize:
  With you within my heart I rise in rate,
  Just as a gem engraved with delicate
  Devices o'er the uncut stone doth rise;
Or as a painted sheet exceeds in price
  Each leaf left pure and in its virgin state:
  Such then am I since I was consecrate
  To be the mark for arrows from your eyes.
Stamped with your seal I'm safe where'er I go,
  Like one who carries charms or coat of mail
  Against all dangers that his life assail.
Nor fire nor water now may work me woe;
  Sight to the blind I can restore by you,
  Heal every wound, and every loss renew.

XX.

THE GARLAND AND THE GIRDLE.

Quanto si gode, lieta.

WHAT *joy hath yon glad wreath of flowers that is*
 Around her golden hair so deftly twined,
 Each blossom pressing forward from behind,
 As though to be the first her brows to kiss!
The livelong day her dress hath perfect bliss,
 That now reveals her breast, now seems to bind:
 And that fair woven net of gold refined
 Rests on her cheek and throat in happiness!
Yet still more blissful seems to me the band,
 Gilt at the tips, so sweetly doth it ring,
 And clasp the bosom that it serves to lace:
Yea, and the belt, to such as understand,
 Bound round her waist, saith: Here I'd ever cling!
 What would my arms do in that girdle's place?

XXI.

THE SILKWORM.

D' altrui pietoso.

Kind to the world, but to itself unkind,
 A worm is born, that, dying noiselessly,
 Despoils itself to clothe fair limbs, and be
In its true worth alone by death divined.
Would I might die for my dear lord to find
 Raiment in my outworn mortality:
 That, changing like the snake, I might be free
To cast the slough wherein I dwell confined!
Nay, were it mine, that shaggy fleece that stays,
 Woven and wrought into a vestment fair,
 Around yon breast so beauteous in such bliss!
All through the day thou'd clasp me! Would I were
 The shoes that bear that burden! when the ways
 Were wet with rain, thy feet I then should kiss!

XXII.

WAITING IN FAITH.

Se nel volto per gli occhi.

IF through the eyes the heart speaks clear and true,
  I have no stronger sureties than these eyes
    For my pure love. Prithee let them suffice,
    Lord of my soul, pity to gain from you.
More tenderly perchance than is my due,
    Your spirit sees into my heart, where rise
    The flames of holy worship, nor denies
    The grace reserved for those who humbly sue.
Oh, blessèd day when you at last are mine!
    Let time stand still, and let noon's chariot stay;
    Fixed be that moment on the dial of heaven!
That I may clasp and keep, by grace divine,
    Clasp in these yearning arms and keep for aye
My heart's loved lord to me desertless given!

XXIII.

FLESH AND SPIRIT.

Ben posson gli occhi.

WELL *may these eyes of mine both near and far*
Behold the beams that from thy beauty flow;
But, lady, feet must halt where sight may go:
We see, but cannot climb to clasp a star.
The pure ethereal soul surmounts that bar
Of flesh, and soars to where thy splendours glow,
Free through the eyes; while prisoned here below,
Though fired with fervent love, our bodies are.
Clogged with mortality and wingless, we
Cannot pursue an angel in her flight:
Only to gaze exhausts our utmost might.
Yet, if but heaven like earth incline to thee,
Let my whole body be one eye to see,
That not one part of me may miss thy sight!

XXIV.

THE DOOM OF BEAUTY.

Spirto ben nato.

CHOICE *soul, in whom, as in a glass, we see,*
   Mirrored in thy pure form and delicate,
   What beauties heaven and nature can create,
   The paragon of all their works to be !
Fair soul, in whom love, pity, piety,
   Have found a home, as from thy outward state
   We clearly read, and are so rare and great
   That they adorn none other like to thee !
Love takes me captive ; beauty binds my soul ;
   Pity and mercy with their gentle eyes
   Wake in my heart a hope that cannot cheat.
What law, what destiny, what fell control,
   What cruelty, or late or soon, denies
   That death should spare perfection so complete ?

XXV.

THE TRANSFIGURATION OF BEAUTY:

A DIALOGUE WITH LOVE.

Dimmi di grazia, amor.

N AY, *prithee tell me, Love, when I behold*
My lady, do mine eyes her beauty see
In truth, or dwells that loveliness in me
Which multiplies her grace a thousandfold?
Thou needs must know; for thou with her of old
Comest to stir my soul's tranquillity;
Yet would I not seek one sigh less, or be
By loss of that loved flame more simply cold.—
The beauty thou discernest, all is hers;
But grows in radiance as it soars on high
Through mortal eyes unto the soul above:
'Tis there transfigured; for the soul confers
On what she holds, her own divinity:
And this transfigured beauty wins thy love.

XXVI.

JOY MAY KILL.

Non men gran grazia, donna.

Too much good luck no less than misery
    May kill a man condemned to mortal pain,
    If, lost to hope and chilled in every vein,
    A sudden pardon comes to set him free.
Thus thy unwonted kindness shown to me
    Amid the gloom where only sad thoughts reign,
    With too much rapture bringing light again,
    Threatens my life more than that agony.
Good news and bad may bear the self-same knife ;
    And death may follow both upon their flight ;
    For hearts that shrink or swell, alike will break.
Let then thy beauty, to preserve my life,
    Temper the source of this supreme delight,
    Lest joy so poignant slay a soul so weak.

XXVII.

NO ESCAPE FROM LOVE.

Non posso altra figura.

I CANNOT *by the utmost flight of thought*
  Conceive another form of air or clay,
    Wherewith against thy beauty to array
    My wounded heart in armour fancy-wrought :
For, lacking thee, so low my state is brought,
    That Love hath stolen all my strength away ;
    Whence, when I fain would halve my griefs,
      they weigh
    With double sorrow, and I sink to nought.
Thus all in vain my soul to scape thee flies,
    For ever faster flies her beauteous foe :
    From the swift-footed feebly run the slow !
Yet with his hands Love wipes my weeping eyes,
    Saying, this toil will end in happy cheer ;
    What costs the heart so much, must needs **be dear** *!*

XXVIII.

THE HEAVENLY BIRTH OF LOVE AND BEAUTY.

La vita del mie amor.

THIS *heart of flesh feeds not with life my love :*
  The love wherewith I love thee hath no heart ;
  Nor harbours it in any mortal part,
  Where erring thought or ill desire may move.
When first Love sent our souls from God above,
  He fashioned me to see thee as thou art —
  Pure light ; and thus I find God's counterpart
  In thy fair face, and feel the sting thereof.
As heat from fire, from loveliness divine
  The mind that worships what recalls the sun
  From whence she sprang, can be divided never :
And since thine eyes all Paradise enshrine,
  Burning unto those orbs of light I run,
  There where I loved thee first to dwell for ever.

XXIX.

LOVE'S DILEMMA.

I' mi credetti.

I DEEMED *upon that day when first I knew*
  So many peerless beauties blent in one,
    That, like an eagle gazing on the sun,
    Mine eyes might fix on the least part of you.
That dream hath vanished, and my hope is flown;
  For he who fain a seraph would pursue
    Wingless, hath cast words to the winds, and dew
    On stones, and gauged God's reason with his own.
If then my heart cannot endure the blaze
    Of beauties infinite that blind these eyes,
    Nor yet can bear to be from you divided,
What fate is mine? Who guides or guards my ways,
    Seeing my soul, so lost and ill-betided,
    Burns in your presence, in your absence dies?

XXX.

LOVE THE LIGHT-GIVER.

TO TOMMASO DE' CAVALIERI.

Veggio co' bei vostri occhi.

With your fair eyes a charming light I see,
 For which my own blind eyes would peer in vain;
 Stayed by your feet, the burden I sustain
 Which my lame feet find all too strong for me;
Wingless upon your pinions forth I fly;
 Heavenward your spirit stirreth me to strain;
 E'en as you will, I blush and blanch **again**,
 Freeze in the sun, burn 'neath a frosty sky.
Your will includes and is the lord of mine;
 Life to my thoughts within your heart is given;
 My words begin to breathe upon your breath:
Like to the moon am I, that cannot shine
 Alone; for lo! our eyes see nought in heaven
 Save what the living sun illumineth.

XXXI.

LOVE'S LORDSHIP.

TO TOMMASO DE' CAVALIERI.

A che più debb' io.

WHY should I seek to ease intense desire
  With still more tears and windy words of grief,
  When heaven, or late or soon, sends no relief
  To souls whom love hath robed around with fire?
Why need my aching heart to death aspire,
  When all must die? Nay, death beyond belief
  Unto these eyes would be both sweet and brief,
  Since in my sum of woes all joys expire!
Therefore, because I cannot shun the blow
  I rather seek, say who must rule my breast,
  Gliding between her gladness and her woe?
If only chains and bands can make me blest,
  No marvel if alone and bare I go,
  An arméd KNIGHT'S captive and slave confessed.

XXXII.

LOVE'S EXPOSTULATION.

S' un casto amor.

I<small>F</small> *love be chaste, if virtue conquer ill,*
   If fortune bind both lovers in one bond,
     If either at the other's grief despond,
     If both be governed by one life, one will;
If in two bodies one soul triumph still,
   Raising the twain from earth to heaven beyond,
   If Love with one blow and one golden wand
   Have power both smitten breasts to pierce
      and thrill;
If each the other love, himself forgoing,
   With such delight, such savour, and so well,
   That both to one sole end their wills combine;
If thousands of these thoughts, all thought outgoing,
   Fail the least part of their firm love to tell:
   Say, can mere angry spite this knot untwine?

XXXIII.

A PRAYER TO NATURE.

AMOR REDIVIVUS.

Perchè tuo gran bellezze.

That *thy great beauty on our earth may be*
    Shrined in a lady softer and more kind,
    I call on nature to collect and bind
    All those delights the slow years steal from thee,
And save them to restore the radiancy
    Of thy bright face in some fair form designed
    By heaven; and may love ever bear in mind
    To mould her heart of grace and courtesy.
I call on nature too to keep my sighs,
    My scattered tears to take and recombine,
    And give to him who loves that fair again:
More happy he perchance shall move those eyes
    To mercy by the griefs wherewith I pine,
    Nor lose the kindness that from me is ta'en!

XXXIII.

A PRAYER TO NATURE.

AMOR REDIVIVUS.

Sol perchè tue bellezze.

IF only that thy beauties here may be
    Deathless through Time that rends the wreaths
        he twined,
      I trust that Nature will collect and bind
      All those delights the slow years steal from thee,
And keep them for a birth more happily
      Born under better auspices, refined
      Into a heavenly form of nobler mind,
      And dowered with all thine angel purity.
Ah me! and may heaven also keep my sighs,
      My scattered tears preserve and reunite,
      And give to him who loves that fair again!
More happy he perchance shall move those eyes
      To mercy by the griefs my manhood blight,
      Nor lose the kindness that from me is ta'en!

XXXIV.

LOVE'S FURNACE.

Sì amico al freddo sasso.

So friendly is the fire to flinty stone,
    That, struck therefrom and kindled to a blaze,
    It burns the stone, and from the ash doth raise
    What lives thenceforward binding stones in one :
Kiln-hardened this resists both frost and sun,
    Acquiring higher worth for endless days —
    As the purged soul from hell returns with praise,
    Amid the heavenly host to take her throne.
E'en so the fire struck from my soul, that lay
    Close-hidden in my heart, may temper me,
    Till burned and slaked to better life I rise.
If, made mere smoke and dust, I live to-day,
    Fire-hardened I shall live eternally ;
    Such gold, not iron, my spirit strikes and tries.

XXXV.

LOVE'S PARADOXES.

Sento d' un foco.

FAR off with fire I feel a cold face lit,
    That makes me burn, the while itself doth freeze:
    Two fragile arms enchain me, which with ease,
    Unmoved themselves, can move weights infinite
A soul none knows but I, most exquisite,
    That, deathless, deals me death, my spirit sees:
    I meet with one who, free, my heart doth seize:
    And who alone can cheer, hath tortured it.
How can it be that from one face like thine
    My own should feel effects so contrary,
    Since ill comes not from things devoid of ill?
That loveliness perchance doth make me pine,
    Even as the sun, whose fiery beams we see,
    Inflames the world, while he is temperate still.

XXXVI.

LOVE MISINTERPRETED.

Se l'immortal desio.

IF the undying thirst that purifies
 Our mortal thoughts, could draw mine to the day,
  Perchance the lord who now holds cruel sway
  In Love's high house, would prove more kindly-
   wise.
But since the laws of heaven immortalise
  Our souls, and doom our flesh to swift decay,
  Tongue cannot tell how fair, how pure as day,
  Is the soul's thirst that far beyond it lies.
How then, ah woe is me! shall that chaste fire,
  Which burns the heart within me, be made known,
  If sense finds only sense in what it sees?
All my fair hours are turned to miseries
  With my loved lord, who minds but lies alone;
  For, truth to tell, who trusts not is a liar.

.

XXXVII.

LOVE'S SERVITUDE.

PERHAPS TO VITTORIA COLONNA.

S' alcun legato è pur.

He who is bound by some great benefit,
  As to be raised from death to life again,
  How shall he recompense that gift, or gain
  Freedom from servitude so infinite?
Yet if 't were possible to pay the debt,
  He'd lose that kindness which we entertain
  For those who serve us well; since it is plain
  That kindness needs some boon to quicken it.
Wherefore, O lady, to maintain thy grace,
  So far above my fortune, what I bring
  Is rather thanklessness than courtesy:
For if both met as equals face to face,
  She whom I love could not be called my king;—
  There is no lordship in equality.

xlix

XXXVIII.

LOVE'S VAIN EXPENSE.

Rendete a gli occhi miei.

G IVE *back unto mine eyes, ye fount and rill,*
  Those streams, not yours, that are so full and
    strong,
  That swell your springs, and roll your waves along
  With force unwonted in your native hill!
And thou, dense air, weighed with my sighs so chill,
  That hidest heaven's own light thick mists among,
  Give back those sighs to my sad heart, nor wrong
  My visual ray with thy dark face of ill!
Let earth give back the footprints that I wore,
  That the bare grass I spoiled may sprout again;
  And Echo, now grown deaf, my cries return!
Loved eyes, unto mine eyes those looks restore,
  And let me woo another not in vain,
  Since how to please thee I shall never learn!

1

LOVE'S ARGUMENT WITH REASON.

La ragion meco si lamenta.

R EASON *laments and grieves full sore with me,*
   The while I hope by loving to be blest ;
   With precepts sound and true philosophy
   My shame she quickens thus within my breast :
' What else but death will that sun deal to thee —
   Nor like the phœnix in her flaming nest ?'
   Yet nought avails this wise morality ;
   No hand can save a suicide confessed.
I know my doom ; the truth I apprehend :
   But on the other side my traitorous heart
   Slays me whene'er to wisdom's words I bend.
Between two deaths my lady stands apart :
   This death I dread ; that none can comprehend.
   In this suspense body and soul must part.

LOVE'S LOADSTONE.

No so s' è la desiata luce.

I KNOW *not if it be the longed-for light*
  Of her first Maker which the spirit feels;
    Or if a time-old memory reveals
    Some other beauty for the heart's delight;
Or fame or dreams beget that vision bright,
    Sweet to the eyes, which through the bosom steals,
    Leaving I know not what that wounds and heals,
    And now perchance hath made me weep outright.
Be this what this may be, 't is this I seek:
    Nor guide have I; nor know I where to find
    That burning fire; yet some one seems to lead.
This, since I saw thee, lady, makes me weak;
    A bitter-sweet sways here and there my mind,
    And sure I am thine eyes this mischief breed.

XL.

LOVE'S LOADSTONE.

Non so se s' è l' immaginata luce.

I KNOW *not if it be the fancied light*
  Which every man or more or less doth feel;
    Or if the mind and memory reveal
    Some other beauty for the heart's delight;
Or if within the soul the vision bright
    Of her celestial home once more doth steal,
    Drawing our better thoughts with pure appeal
    To the true Good above all mortal sight:
This light I long for and unguided seek;
    This fire that burns my heart, I cannot find;
    Nor know the way, though some one seems to lead.
This, since I saw thee, lady, makes me weak:
    A bitter-sweet sways here and there my mind;
    And sure I am thine eyes this mischief breed.

XLI.

LIGHT AND DARKNESS.

Colui che fece.

He who ordained, when first the world began,
    Time, that was not before creation's hour,
    Divided it, and gave the sun's high power
    To rule the one, the moon the other span:
Thence fate and changeful chance and fortune's ban
    Did in one moment down on mortals shower:
    To me they portioned darkness for a dower;
    Dark hath my lot been since I was a man.
Myself am ever mine own counterfeit;
    And as deep night grows still more dim and dun,
    So still of more misdoing must I rue:
Meanwhile this solace to my soul is sweet,
    That my black night doth make more clear the sun
    Which at your birth was given to wait on you.

XLII.

SACRED NIGHT.

Ogni van chiuso.

ALL *hollow vaults and dungeons sealed from sight,*
    All caverns circumscribed with roof and wall,
    Defend dark Night, though noon around her fall,
    From the fierce play of solar day-beams bright.
But if she be assailed by fire or light,
    Her powers divine are nought ; they tremble all
    Before things far more vile and trivial —
    Even a glow-worm can confound their might.
The earth that lies bare to the sun, and breeds
    A thousand germs that burgeon and decay —
    This earth is wounded by the ploughman's share :
But only darkness serves for human seeds ;
    Night therefore is more sacred far than day,
    Since man excels all fruits however fair.

XLIII.

THE IMPEACHMENT OF NIGHT.

Perchè Febo non torce.

WHAT time bright *Phœbus* doth not stretch and bend
His shining arms around this terrene sphere,
The people call that season dark and drear
Night, for the cause they do not comprehend.
So weak is *Night* that if our hand extend
A glimmering torch, her shadows disappear,
Leaving her dead; like frailest gossamere,
Tinder and steel her mantle rive and rend.
Nay, if this Night be anything at all,
Sure she is daughter of the sun and earth;
This holds, the other spreads that shadowy pall.
Howbeit they err who praise this gloomy birth,
So frail and desolate and void of mirth
That one poor firefly can her might appal.

XLIV.

THE DEFENCE OF NIGHT.

O nott' o dolce tempo.

O NIGHT, *O sweet though sombre span of time !—*
All things find rest upon their journey's end—
Whoso hath praised thee, well doth apprehend ;
And whoso honours thee, hath wisdom's prime.
Our *cares thou canst to quietude sublime ;*
For dews and darkness are of peace the friend :
Often by thee in dreams upborne, I wend
From earth to heaven, where yet I hope to climb.
Thou shade *of Death, through whom the soul at length*
Shuns pain and sadness hostile to the heart,
Whom mourners find their last and sure relief !
Thou *dost restore our suffering flesh to strength,*
Driest our tears, assuagest every smart,
Purging the spirits of the pure from grief.

.

XLV.

LOVE FEEDS THE FLAME OF AGE.

Quand' il servo il signior.

WHEN *masters bind a slave with cruel chain,*
And keep him hope-forlorn in bondage pent,
Use tames his temper to imprisonment,
And hardly would he fain be free again.
Use curbs the snake and tiger, and doth train
Fierce woodland lions to bear chastisement;
And the young artist, all with toil forspent,
By constant use a giant's strength doth gain.
But with the force of flame it is not so:
For while fire sucks the sap of the green wood,
It warms a frore old man and makes him grow;
With such fine heat of youth and lustihood
Filling his heart and teaching it to glow,
That love enfolds him with beatitude.
If then in playful mood
He sport and jest, old age need no man blame;
For loving things divine implies no shame.
The soul that knows her aim,
Sins not by loving God's own counterfeit—
Due measure kept, and bounds, and order meet.

lviii

XLVI.

LOVE'S FLAME DOTH FEED ON AGE.

Se da' prim' anni.

If some mild heat of love in youth confessed
   'Burns a fresh heart with swift consuming fire,
      What will the force be of a flame more dire
      Shut up within an old man's cindery breast?
If the mere lapse of lengthening years hath pressed
      So sorely that life, strength, and vigour tire,
      How shall he fare who must ere long expire,
      When to old age is added love's unrest?
Weak as myself, he will be whirled away
      Like dust by winds kind in their cruelty,
      Robbing the loathly worm of its last prey.
A little flame consumed and fed on me
      In my green age : now that the wood is dry,
      What hope against this fire more fierce have I?

XLVII.

BEAUTY'S INTOLERABLE SPLENDOUR.

Se 'l foco alla bellezza.

IF but the fire that lightens in thine eyes
   Were equal with their beauty, all the snow
      And frost of all the world would melt and glow
      Like brands that blaze beneath fierce tropic skies.
But heaven in mercy to our miseries
   Dulls and divides the fiery beams that flow
      From thy great loveliness, that we may go
      Through this stern mortal life in tranquil wise.
Thus beauty burns not with consuming rage;
   For so much only of the heavenly light
      Inflames our love as finds a fervent heart.
This is my case, lady, in sad old age:
   If seeing thee, I do not die outright,
      'Tis that I feel thy beauty but in part.

.

.

.

XLVIII.

LOVE'S EVENING.

Se 'l troppo indugio.

WHAT though long waiting wins more happiness
  Than petulant desire is wont to gain,
    My luck in latest age hath brought me pain,
    Thinking how brief must be an old man's bliss.
Heaven, if it heed our lives, can hardly bless
    This fire of love when frosts are wont to reign :
    For so I love thee, lady, and my strain
    Of tears through age exceeds in tenderness.
Yet peradventure though my day is done,—
    Though nearly past the setting mid thick cloud
    And frozen exhalations sinks my sun,—
If love to only mid-day be allowed,
    And I an old man in my evening burn,
    You, lady, still my night to noon may turn.

XLIX.

LOVE'S EXCUSE.

Dal dolcie pianto.

FROM *happy tears to woeful smiles, from peace*
    Eternal to a brief and hollow truce,
    How have I fallen!—when 't is truth we lose,
    Sense triumphs o'er all adverse impulses.
I know not if my heart bred this disease,
    That still more pleasing grows with growing use;
    Or else thy face, thine eyes, which stole the hues
    And fires of Paradise—less fair than these.
Thy beauty is no mortal thing; 't was sent
    From heaven on high to make our earth divine:
    Wherefore, though wasting, burning, I'm content;
For in thy sight what could I do but pine?
    If God himself thus rules my destiny,
    Who, when I die, can lay the blame on thee?

L.

IN LOVE'S OWN TIME.

S' i' avessi creduto.

HAD I but earlier known that from the eyes
 Of that bright soul that fires me like the sun,
 I might have drawn new strength my race to run,
 'Burning as burns the phœnix ere it dies;
Even as the stag or lynx or leopard flies
 To seek his pleasure and his pain to shun,
 Each word, each smile of her would I have won,
 Flying where now sad age all flight denies.
Yet why complain? For even now I find
 In that glad angel's face, so full of rest,
 Health and content, heart's ease and peace of mind
Perchance I might have been less simply blest,
 Finding her sooner: if 'tis age alone
 That lets me soar with her to seek God's throne.

LI.

LOVE IN YOUTH AND AGE.

Tornami al tempo.

Bring back the time when blind desire ran free,
  With bit and rein too loose to curb his flight;
  Give back the buried face, once angel-bright,
  That hides in earth all comely things from me;
Bring back those journeys ta'en so toilsomely,
  So toilsome-slow to one whose hairs are white;
  Those tears and flames that in one breast unite;
  If thou wilt once more take thy fill of me!
Yet Love! Suppose it true that thou dost thrive
  Only on bitter honey-dews of tears,
  Small profit hast thou of a weak old man.
My soul that toward the other shore doth strive,
  Wards off thy darts with shafts of holier fears;
  And fire feeds ill on brands no breath can fan.

lxiv

LI.

LOVE IN YOUTH AND AGE.

Tornami al tempo.

B RING *back the time when glad desire ran free*
    With bit and rein too loose to curb his flight,
    The tears and flames that in one breast unite,
    If thou art fain once more to conquer me!
Bring back those journeys ta'en so toilsomely,
    So toilsome-slow to him whose hairs are white!
    Give back the buried face once angel-bright,
    That taxed all Nature's art and industry.
O Love! an old man finds it hard to chase
    Thy flying pinions!   Thou hast left thy nest;
    Nor is my heart as light as heretofore.
Put thy gold arrows to the string once more:
    Then if Death hear my prayer and grant me grace,
    My grief I shall forget, again made blest.

lxv

LII.

CELESTIAL LOVE.

Non vider gli occhi miei.

I SAW *no mortal beauty with these eyes*
  When perfect peace in thy fair eyes I found;
    But far within, where all is holy ground,
    My soul felt Love, her comrade of the skies:
For she was born with God in Paradise;
    Else should we still to transient love be bound;
    But, finding these so false, we pass beyond
    Unto the Love of loves that never dies.
Nay, things that die cannot assuage the thirst
    Of souls undying; nor Eternity
    Serves Time, where all must fade that flourisheth.
Sense is not love, but lawlessness accurst:
    This kills the soul; while our love lifts on high
    Our friends on earth — higher in heaven through
      death.

LIII.

CELESTIAL AND EARTHLY LOVE.

Non è sempre di colpa.

LOVE *is not always harsh and deadly sin,*
  When love for boundless beauty makes us pine ;
  The heart, by love left soft and infantine,
  Will let the shafts of God's grace enter in.
Love wings and wakes the soul, stirs her to win
  Her flight aloft, nor e'er to earth decline ;
  'T is the first step that leads her to the shrine
  Of Him who slakes the thirst that burns within.
The love of that whereof I speak ascends :
  Woman is different far ; the love of her
  But ill befits a heart manly and wise.
The one love soars, the other earthward tends ;
  The soul lights this, while that the senses stir ;
  And still lust's arrow at base quarry flies.

LIV.

LOVE LIFTS TO GOD.

Veggio nel tuo bel viso.

FROM *thy fair face I learn, O my loved lord,*
   That which no mortal tongue can rightly say;
   The soul imprisoned in her house of clay,
Holpen by thee, to God hath often soared.
And though the vulgar, vain, malignant horde
   Attribute what their grosser wills obey,
   Yet shall this fervent homage that I pay,
   *This love, **this faith**, pure joys for us afford.*
Lo, all the lovely things we find on earth,
   Resemble for the soul that rightly sees
   That *source of bliss divine which gave us birth :*
Nor have we first-fruits or remembrances
   Of heaven elsewhere.   Thus, loving loyally,
   I rise to God, and make death sweet by thee.

LV.

LOVE'S ENTREATY.

Tu sa' ch' i' so, Signor mie.

THOU *knowest, love, I know that thou dost know*
  That I am here more near to thee to be,
  And knowest that I know thou knowest me :
  What means it then that we are sundered so ?
If they are true, these hopes that from thee flow,
  If it is real, this sweet expectancy,
  Break down the wall that stands 'twixt me and thee ;
  For pain in prison pent hath double woe.
Because in thee I love, O my loved lord,
  What thou best lovest, be not therefore stern :
  Souls burn for souls, spirits to spirits cry !
I seek the splendour in thy fair face stored ;
  Yet living man that beauty scarce can learn,
  And he who fain would find it, first must die.

LVI.

HEAVEN-BORN BEAUTY.

Per ritornar là.

A s one who will re-seek her home of light,
    Thy form immortal to this prison-house
    Descended, like an angel piteous,
    To heal all hearts and make the whole world bright.
'T is this that thralls my soul in love's delight,
    Not thy clear face of beauty glorious;
    For he who harbours virtue, still will choose
    To love what neither years nor death can blight.
So fares it ever with things high and rare
    Wrought in the sweat of nature; heaven above
    Showers on their birth the blessings of her prime:
Nor hath God deigned to show Himself elsewhere
    More clearly than in human forms sublime,
    Which, since they image Him, alone I love.

LVI.

HEAVEN-BORN BEAUTY.

Venne, non so ben donde.

I*t came, I know not whence, from far above,*
  That clear immortal flame that still doth rise
    Within thy sacred breast, and fills the skies,
    And heals all hearts, and adds to heaven new love.
This burns me, this, and the pure light thereof;
    Not thy fair face, thy sweet untroubled eyes:
    For love that is not love for aught that dies,
    Dwells in the soul where no base passions move.
If then such loveliness upon its own
    Should graft new beauties in a mortal birth,
    'The sheath bespeaks the shining blade within.
To gain our love God hath not clearer shown
    Himself elsewhere: thus heaven doth vie with earth
    To make thee worthy worship without sin.

LVII.

CARNAL AND SPIRITUAL LOVE.

Passa per gli occhi.

S WIFT *through the eyes unto the heart within*
All lovely forms that thrall our spirit stray;
So smooth and broad and open is the way
That thousands and not hundreds enter in.
Burdened with scruples and weighed down with sin,
These mortal beauties fill me with dismay;
Nor find I one that doth not strive to stay
My soul on transient joy, or lets me win
The heaven I yearn for.   Lo, when erring love—
Who fills the world, howe'er his power we shun,
Else were the world a grave and we undone—
Assails the soul, if grace refuse to fan
Our purged desires and make them soar above,
What grief it were to have been born a man!

LVII.

CARNAL AND SPIRITUAL LOVE.

Passa per gli occhi.

S WIFT *through the eyes unto the heart within*
 All lovely forms that thrall our spirit stray ;
 So smooth and broad and open is the way
 That thousands and not hundreds enter in
Of every age and sex : whence I begin,
 Burdened with griefs, but more with dull dismay,
 To fear ; nor find mid all their bright array
 One that with full content my heart may win.
If mortal beauty be the food of love,
 It came not with the soul from heaven, and thus
 That love itself must be a mortal fire :
But if love reach to nobler hopes above,
 Thy love shall scorn me not nor dread desire
 That seeks a carnal prey assailing us.

LVIII.

LOVE AND DEATH.

Ognor che l' idol mio.

WHENE'ER *the idol of these eyes appears*
  Unto my musing heart so weak and strong,
    Death comes between her and my soul ere long
    Chasing her thence with troops of gathering fears.
Nathless this violence my spirit cheers
  With better hope than if she had no wrong;
    While Love invincible arrays the throng
    Of dauntless thoughts, and thus harangues his peers:
But once, he argues, can a mortal die;
  But once be born: and he who dies afire,
    What shall he gain if erst he dwelt with me?
That burning love whereby the soul flies free,
  Doth lure each fervent spirit to aspire
    Like gold refined in flame to God on high.

LIX.

LOVE IS A REFINER'S FIRE.

Non più ch' 'l foco il fabbro.

IT *is with fire that blacksmiths iron subdue*
   Unto fair form, the image of their thought :
      Nor without fire hath any artist wrought
      Gold to its utmost purity of hue.
Nay, nor the unmatched phœnix lives anew,
   Unless she burn : if then I am distraught
      By fire, I may to better life be brought
      Like those whom death restores nor years undo.
The fire whereof I speak, is my great cheer ;
      Such power it hath to renovate and raise
      Me who was almost numbered with the dead ;
And since by nature fire doth find its sphere
      Soaring aloft, and I am all ablaze,
      Heavenward with it my flight must needs be sped.

LX.

LOVE'S JUSTIFICATION.

Ben può talor col mio.

SOMETIMES *my love I dare to entertain*
With soaring hope not over-credulous;
Since if all human loves were impious,
Unto what end did God the world ordain?
For loving thee what license is more plain
Than that I praise thereby the glorious
Source of all joys divine, that comfort us
In thee, and with chaste fires our soul sustain?
False hope belongs unto that love alone
Which with declining beauty wanes and dies,
And, like the face it worships, fades away.
That hope is true which the pure heart hath known,
Which alters not with time or death's decay,
Yielding on earth earnest of Paradise.

LX.

LOVE'S JUSTIFICATION.

Ben può talor col casto.

IT must be right sometimes to entertain
  Chaste love with hope not over-credulous;
    Since if all human loves were impious,
    Unto what end did God the world ordain?
If I love thee and bend beneath thy reign,
    'T is for the sake of beauty glorious
    Which in thine eyes divine is stored for us,
    And drives all evil thought from its domain.
That is not love whose tyranny we own
    In loveliness that every moment dies;
    Which, like the face it worships, fades away:
True love is that which the pure heart hath known,
    Which alters not with time or death's decay,
    Yielding on earth earnest of Paradise.

LXI.

IRREPARABLE LOSS.

AFTER THE DEATH OF VITTORIA COLONNA.

Se 'l mie rozzo martello.

WHEN *my rude hammer to the stubborn stone*
Gives human shape, now that, now this, at will,
Following his hand who wields and guides it still,
It moves upon another's feet alone :
But that which dwells in heaven, the world doth fill
With beauty by pure motions of its own ;
And since tools fashion tools which else were none,
Its life makes all that lives with living skill.
Now, for that every stroke excels the more
The higher at the forge it doth ascend,
Her soul that fashioned mine hath sought the skies :
Wherefore unfinished I must meet my end,
If God, the great Artificer, denies
That aid which was unique on earth before.

LXII.

LOVE'S TRIUMPH OVER DEATH.

AFTER THE DEATH OF VITTORIA COLONNA.

Quand' el ministro de' sospir.

WHEN she who was the source of all my sighs,
    Fled from the world, herself, my straining sight,
    Nature who gave us that unique delight,
    Was sunk in shame, and we had weeping eyes.
Yet shall not vauntful Death enjoy this prize,
    This sun of suns which then he veiled in night;
    For Love hath triumphed, lifting up her light
On earth and 'mid the saints in Paradise.
    What though remorseless and impiteous doom
    Deemed that the music of her deeds would die,
    And that her splendour would be sunk in gloom?
The poet's page exalts her to the sky
    With life more living in the lifeless tomb,
    And Death translates her soul to reign on high.

LXIII.

AFTER SUNSET.

AFTER THE DEATH OF VITTORIA COLONNA.

Be' mi dove'.

WELL *might I in those days so fortunate,*
  What time the sun lightened my path above,
  Have soared from earth to heaven, raised by her love
  Who winged my labouring soul and sweetened fate.
That sun hath set; and I with hope elate
  Who deemed that those bright days would never move,
  Find that my thankless soul, deprived thereof,
  Declines to death, while heaven still bars the gate.
Love lent me wings; my path was like a stair;
  A lamp unto my feet, that sun was given;
  And death was safety and great joy to find.
But dying now, I shall not climb to heaven;
  Nor can mere memory cheer my heart's despair:—
  What help remains when hope is left behind?

lxxx

LXIV.

A WASTED BRAND.

AFTER THE DEATH OF VITTORIA COLONNA.

Qual maraviglia è.

I F *being near the fire I burned with it,*
  Now that its flame is quenched and doth not show,
    What wonder if I waste within and glow,
    Dwindling away to cinders bit by bit?
While still it burned, I saw so brightly lit
    That splendour whence I drew my grievous woe,
    That from its sight alone could pleasure flow,
    And death and torment both seemed exquisite.
But now that heaven hath robbed me of the blaze
    Of that great fire which burned and nourished me,
    A coal that smoulders 'neath the ash am I.
Unless Love furnish wood fresh flames to raise,
    I shall expire with not one spark to see,
    So quickly into embers do I die!

LXV.

ON THE BRINK OF DEATH.

TO GIORGIO VASARI.

Giunto è già.

Now hath my life across a stormy sea,
    Like a frail bark, reached that wide port where all
    Are bidden, ere the final reckoning fall
Of good and evil for eternity.
Now know I well how that fond phantasy
    Which made my soul the worshipper and thrall
    Of earthly art is vain; how criminal
Is that which all men seek unwillingly.
Those amorous thoughts which were so lightly dressed,
    What are they when the double death is nigh?
    The one I know for sure, the other dread.
Painting nor sculpture now can lull to rest
    My soul, that turns to His great love on high,
    Whose arms to clasp us on the cross were spread.

VANITY OF VANITIES.

TO GIORGIO VASARI.

Le favole del mondo.

THE *fables of the world have filched away*
 The time I had for thinking upon God;
 His grace lies buried 'neath oblivion's sod,
 Whence springs an evil crop of sins alway.
What makes another wise, leads me astray,
 Slow to discern the bad path I have trod:
 Hope fades, but still desire ascends that God
 May free me from self-love, my sure decay.
Shorten half-way my road to heaven from earth!
 Dear Lord, I cannot even half-way rise
 Unless Thou help me on this pilgrimage.
Teach me to hate the world so little worth,
 And all the lovely things I clasp and prize,
 That endless life, ere death, may be my wage.

.

LXVII.

A PRAYER FOR FAITH.

Non è più bassa.

THERE'S *not on earth a thing more vile and base*
    Than, lacking Thee, I feel myself to be :
    For pardon prays my own debility,
    Yearning in vain to lift me to Thy face.
Stretch to me, Lord, that chain whose links enlace
    All heavenly gifts and all felicity —
    Faith, whereunto I strive perpetually,
    Yet cannot find (my fault) her perfect grace.
That gift of gifts, the rarer 't is, the more
    I count it great ; more great, because to earth
    Without it neither peace nor joy is given.
If Thou Thy blood so lovingly didst pour,
    Let not that bounty fail or suffer dearth,
    Withholding Faith that opes the doors of heaven.

LXVIII.

URBINO.

TO MONSIGNOR LODOVICO BECCADELLI.

Per croce e grazia.

GOD'S *grace, the cross, our troubles multiplied,*
  Will make us meet in heaven, full well I know :
    Yet ere we yield our breath on earth below,
    Why need a little solace be denied ?
Though seas and mountains and rough ways divide
    Our feet asunder, neither frost nor snow
    Can make the soul her ancient love forgo ;
    Nor chains nor bonds the wings of thought have tied.
'Borne by these wings, with thee I dwell for aye,
    And weep, and of my dead Urbino talk,
    Who, were he living, now perchance would be —
For so 't was planned — thy guest as well as I.
    Warned by his death, another way I walk
    To meet him where he waits to live with me.

LXIX.

WAITING FOR DEATH.

Di morte certo.

My death must come; but when, I do not know:
Life's short, and little life remains for me:
Fain would my flesh abide; my soul would flee
Heavenward, for still she calls on me to go.
'Blind is the world; and evil here below
O'erwhelms and triumphs over honesty:
The light is quenched; quenched too is bravery:
Lies reign, and truth hath ceased her face to show.
When will that day dawn, Lord, for which he waits
Who trusts in Thee? Lo, this prolonged delay
Destroys all hope and robs the soul of life.
Why streams the light from those celestial gates,
If death prevent the day of grace, and stay
Our souls for ever in the toils of strife?

LXX.

A PRAYER FOR STRENGTH.

Carico d' anni.

Burdened *with years and full of sinfulness,*
    With evil custom grown inveterate,
    Both deaths I dread that close before me wait,
    Yet feed my heart on poisonous thoughts no less.
No strength I find in mine own feebleness
    To change or life or love or use or fate,
    Unless Thy heavenly guidance come, though late,
    Which only helps and stays our nothingness.
'T is not enough, dear Lord, to make me yearn
    For that celestial home, where yet my soul
    May be new made, and not, as erst, of nought :
Nay, ere Thou strip her mortal vestment, turn
    My steps toward the steep ascent, that whole
    And pure before Thy face she may be brought.

LXXI.

A PRAYER FOR PURIFICATION.

Forse perchè d' altrui.

PERCHANCE *that I might learn what pity is,*
 That I might laugh at erring men no more,
 Secure in my own strength as heretofore,
 My soul hath fallen from her state of bliss:
Nor know I under any flag but this
 How fighting I may 'scape those perils sore,
 Or how survive the rout and horrid roar
 Of adverse hosts, if I Thy succour miss.
O flesh! O blood! O cross! O pain extreme!
 By you may those foul sins be purified,
 Wherein my fathers were, and I was born!
Lo, Thou alone art good: let Thy supreme
 Pity my state of evil cleanse and hide—
 So near to death, so far from God, forlorn.

LXXII.

A PRAYER FOR AID.

Deh fammiti vedere.

OH, make me see Thee, Lord, where'er I go!
 If mortal beauty sets my soul on fire,
 That flame when near to Thine must needs expire,
 And I with love of only Thee shall glow.
Dear Lord, Thy help I seek against this woe,
 These torments that my spirit vex and tire;
 Thou only with new strength canst re-inspire
 My will, my sense, my courage faint and low.
Thou gavest me on earth this soul divine;
 And Thou within this body weak and frail
 Didst prison it — how sadly there to live!
How can I make its lot less vile than mine?
 Without Thee, Lord, all goodness seems to fail.
 To alter fate is God's prerogative.

LXXIII.

AT THE FOOT OF THE CROSS.

Scarco d' un' importuna.

FREED *from a burden sore and grievous band,*
  Dear Lord, and from this wearying world untied,
  Like a frail bark I turn me to Thy side,
  As from a fierce storm to a tranquil land.
Thy thorns, Thy nails, and either bleeding hand,
  With Thy mild gentle piteous face, provide
  Promise of help and mercies multiplied,
  And hope that yet my soul secure may stand.
Let not Thy holy eyes be just to see
  My evil past, Thy chastened ears to hear
  And stretch the arm of judgment to my crime :
Let Thy blood only lave and succour me,
  Yielding more perfect pardon, better cheer,
  As older still I grow with lengthening time.

LXXIV.

A PRAYER FOR GRACE IN DEATH.

S' avvien che spesso.

WHAT *though strong love of life doth flatter me*
With hope of yet more years on earth to stay,
Death none the less draws nearer day by day,
Who to sad souls alone comes lingeringly.
Yet why desire long life and jollity,
If in our griefs alone to God we pray?
Glad fortune, length of days, and pleasure slay
The soul that trusts to their felicity.
Then if at any hour through grace divine
The fiery shafts of love and faith that cheer
And fortify the soul, my heart assail,
Since nought achieve these mortal powers of mine,
Straight may I wing my way to heaven; for here
With lengthening days good thoughts and wishes fail.

LXXIV.

A PRAYER FOR GRACE IN DEATH.

Parmi che spesso.

OFTTIMES *my great desire doth flatter me*
With hope on earth yet many years to stay :
Still Death, the more I love it, day by day
Takes from the life I love so tenderly.
What better time for that dread change could be,
If in our griefs alone to God we pray ?
Oh, lead me, Lord, oh, lead me far away
From every thought that lures my soul from Thee !
Yea, if at any hour, through grace of Thine,
The fervent zeal of love and faith that cheer
And fortify the soul, my heart assail,
Since nought achieve these mortal powers of mine,
Plant, like a saint in heaven, that virtue here ;
For, lacking Thee, all good must faint and fail.

.

LXXV.

HEART-COLDNESS.

Vorrei voler, Signior.

FAIN *would I wish what my heart cannot will :*
　　Between it and the fire a veil of ice
　　'Deadens the fire, so that I deal in lies ;
　　My words and actions are discordant still.
I love Thee with my tongue, then mourn my fill ;
　　For love warms not my heart, nor can I rise,
　　Or ope the doors of Grace, who from the skies
　　Might flood my soul, and pride and passion kill.
Rend Thou the veil, dear Lord !　'Break Thou that wall
　　Which with its stubbornness retards the rays
　　Of that bright sun this earth hath dulled for me !
Send down Thy promised light to cheer and fall
　　On Thy fair spouse, that I with love may blaze,
　　And, free from doubt, my heart feel only Thee !

LXXVI.

THE DEATH OF CHRIST.

Non fur men lieti.

Not less elate than smitten with wild woe
To see not them but Thee by death undone,
Were those blest souls, when Thou above the sun
Didst raise, by dying, men that lay so low:
Elate, since freedom from all ills that flow
From their first fault for Adam's race was won;
Sore smitten, since in torment fierce God's son
Served servants on the cruel cross below.
Heaven showed she knew Thee, who Thou wert and
whence,
Veiling her eyes above the riven earth;
The mountains trembled and the seas were troubled.
He took the Fathers from Hell's darkness dense:
The torments of the damnéd fiends redoubled:
Man only joyed, who gained baptismal birth.

LXXVII.

THE BLOOD OF CHRIST.

Mentre m' attrista.

MID weariness and woe I find some cheer
 In thinking of the past, when I recall
  My weakness and my sins, and reckon all
  The vain expense of days that disappear :
This cheers by making, ere I die, more clear
 The frailty of what men delight miscall ;
  But saddens me to think how rarely fall
  God's grace and mercies in life's latest year.
For though Thy promises our faith compel,
 Yet, Lord, what man shall venture to maintain
  That pity will condone our long neglect ?
Still from Thy blood poured forth we know full well
 How without measure was Thy martyr's pain,
  How measureless the gifts we dare expect.

NOTES

APPENDICES

NOTES.

I. Quoted by Donato Giannotti in his Dialogue *De' giorni che Dante consumò nel cercare l'Inferno e 'l Purgatorio*. The date of its composition is perhaps 1545.

II. Written probably for Donato Giannotti about the same date.

III. Belonging to the year 1506, when Michael Angelo quarrelled with Julius and left Rome in anger. The tree referred to in the last line is the oak of the Rovere family.

IV. Same date, and same circumstances. The autograph has these words at the foot of the sonnet: *Vostro Miccelangniolo, in Turchia*. Rome itself, the Sacred City, has become a land of infidels.

V. Ser Giovanni da Pistoja was Chancellor of the Florentine Academy. The date is probably 1509. The *Sonetto a Coda* is generally humorous or satiric.

VI. Written in one of those moments of *affanno* or *stizzó* to which the sculptor was subject. For the old bitterness of feeling between Florence and Pistoja, see Dante, *Inferno*, xxiv., xxv.

VII. Michael Angelo was ill during the summer of 1544, and was nursed by Luigi del Riccio in his own house. Shortly after his recovery he quarrelled with his friend, and wrote him this sonnet as well as a very angry letter.

VIII. Cecchino Bracci was a boy of rare and surpassing beauty who died at Rome, January 8, 1544, in his seventeenth year. Besides this sonnet, which refers to a portrait Luigi del Riccio had asked him to make of the dead youth,

Michael Angelo composed a series of forty-eight quatrains upon the same subject, and sent them to his friend Luigi. Michelangelo the younger, thinking that '*l' ignoranzia degli uomini ba campo di mormorare*,' suppressed the name Cecchino and changed *lui* into *lei*. Date about 1544.

IX. Line 4: 'The Archangel's scales alone can weigh my gratitude against your gift.' Lines 5-8: 'Your courtesy has taken away all my power of responding to it. I am as helpless as a ship becalmed, or a wisp of straw on a stormy sea.'

X. Michael Angelo, when asked to make a portrait of his friend's mistress, declares that he is unable to do justice to her beauty. The name *Mancina* is a pun upon the Italian word for the left arm, *Mancino*. This lady was a famous and venal beauty, mentioned among the loves of the poet Molsa.

XI. Date, 1550.

XII. This and the three next sonnets may with tolerable certainty be referred to the series written on various occasions for Vittoria Colonna.

XIII. Sent together with a letter, in which we read: *l' aportatore di questa sarà Urbino, che sta meco.* Urbino was M. A.'s old servant, workman, and friend. See No. LXVIII. and note.

XIV. The thought is that, as the sculptor carves a statue from a rough model by addition and subtraction of the marble, so the lady of his heart refines and perfects his rude native character.

XV. This sonnet is the theme of Varchi's *Lezione*. There is nothing to prove that it was addressed to Vittoria Colonna. Varchi calls it '*un suo altissimo sonetto pieno di quella antica purezza e dantesca gravità*.'

XVI. The thought of the fifteenth is repeated with some variations. His lady's heart holds for the lover good and evil things, according as he has the art to draw them forth.

XVIII. In the terzets he describes the temptations of the artist-nature, over-sensitive to beauty. Michelangelo the younger so **altered these** six lines as to destroy the autobiographical allusion.—Cp. **No.** XXVIII., **note.**

XIX. The lover's heart is like an intaglio, precious by being inscribed with his lady's image.

XX. An early composition, written on the back of a letter sent to the sculptor in Bologna by his brother Simone in 1507. **M. A.** was then **working at the** bronze statue of Julius II. Who the lady of his love was, we do not know. Notice the absence of Platonic *concetti.*

XXIII. It is hardly necessary to call attention to Michael Angelo's oft-recurring Platonism. The thought that the eye alone perceives the **celestial beauty, veiled** beneath the fleshly form of the beloved, **is** repeated in **many** sonnets—especially in XXV., XXVIII.

XXIV. Composed probably in the year 1529.

XXV. Written on the same sheet as the foregoing sonnet, and composed probably in the same year. The **thought** is this: beauty passing from the lady into the lover's soul, is there spiritualised and becomes the object of a spiritual love.

XXVII. **To escape from his** lady, either by interposing another image **of beauty** between the thought of her and his heart, or by **flight, is** impossible.

XXVIII. **Compare Madrigal VII** in illustration of **lines 5 to 8.** By the analogy of that passage, I should venture **to render lines 6 and 7** thus:

> He made thee light, and me the eyes of art;
> Nor fails **my** soul to find God's counterpart.

XXX. Varchi, quoting this sonnet in his *Lezione*, conjectures that it was composed for Tommaso Cavalieri.

XXXI. Varchi asserts without qualification that this sonnet was addressed to Tommaso Cavalieri. The pun in the last line, *Resto prigion d' un Cavalier armato*, seems to me to decide the matter, though Signor Guasti and Signor

Gotti both will have it that a woman must have been
intended. Michelangelo the younger has only left one line,
the second, untouched in his *rifacimento*. Instead of the
last words he gives *un cuor di virtù armato*, being over-
scrupulous for his great-uncle's reputation.

XXXII. Written at the foot of a letter addressed by
Giuliano Bugiardini the painter, from Florence, to M. A. in
Rome, August 5, 1532. This then is probably the date of
the composition.

XXXIV. The metaphor of fire, flint, and mortar breaks
down in the last line, where M. A. forgets that gold cannot
strike a spark from stone.

XXXV. Line 9 has the word *Signor*. It is almost
certain that where M. A. uses this word without further
qualification in a love sonnet, he means his mistress. I
have sometimes translated it 'heart's lord' or 'loved lord,'
because I did not wish to merge the quaintness of this
ancient Tuscan usage in the more commonplace 'lady.'

XXXVI. Line 3: *the lord, etc.* This again is the poet's
mistress. The drift of the sonnet is this: his soul can find
no expression but through speech, and speech is too gross
to utter the purity of his feeling. His mistress again
receives his tongue's message with her ears; and thus
there is an element of sensuality, false and alien to his
intention, both in his complaint and in her acceptation of it.
The last line is a version of the proverb: *chi è avvezzo a
dir bugie, non crede a nessuno.*

XXXVII. At the foot of the sonnet is written *Man-
dato*. The two last lines play on the words *signor* and
signoria. To whom it was sent we do not know for certain;
but we may conjecture Vittoria Colonna.

XXXIX. The paper on which this sonnet is written
has a memorandum with the date January 6, 1529. 'On
my return from Venice, I, Michelagniolo Buonarroti, found
in the house about five loads of straw,' etc. It belongs
therefore to the period of the siege of Florence, when M.

A., as is well known, fled for a short space to Venice. In line 12, I have translated *il mie signiore, my lady.*

XL. No sonnet in the whole collection seems to have cost M. A. so much trouble as this. Besides the two completed versions, which I have rendered, there are several scores of rejected or various readings for single lines in the MSS. The Platonic doctrine of Anamnesis probably supplies the key to the thought which the poet attempted to work out.

XLI., XLII., XLIII., XLIV. There is nothing to prove that these four sonnets on Night were composed in sequence. On the contrary, the personal tone of XLI. seems to separate this from the other three. XLIV. may be accepted as a palinode for XLIII.

XLV., XLVI. Both sonnets deal half humorously with a thought very prominent in M. A.'s compositions — the effect of love on one who is old in years. — Cp. XLVIII., L.

XLVII. The Platonic conception that the pure form of Beauty or of Truth, if seen, would be overwhelming in its brilliancy.

XLIX. The *dolcie pianto* and *eterna pace* are the tears and peace of piety. The *doloroso riso* and *corta pace* are the smiles and happiness of earthly love.

LII. Here is another version of this very beautiful sonnet.

> No mortal thing enthralled these longing eyes
>   When perfect peace in thy fair face I found;
>   But far within, where all is holy ground,
>   My soul felt Love, her comrade of the skies:
> For she was born with God in Paradise;
>   Nor all the shows of beauty shed around
>   This fair false world her wings to earth have bound;
>   Unto the Love of Loves aloft she flies.
> Nay, things that suffer death, quench not the fire
>   Of deathless spirits; nor eternity
>   Serves sordid Time, that withers all things rare.

Not love but lawless impulse is desire:
That slays the soul; our love makes still more fair
Our friends on earth, fairer in death on high.

LIII. This is the doctrine of the Symposium; the scorn of merely sexual love is also Platonic.

LIV. Another sonnet on the theme of the Uranian as distinguished from the Vulgar love. See below, LVI., for a parallel to the second terzet.

LV. The date may be 1532. The play on words in the first quatrain and the first terzet is Shakespearian.

LIX. Two notes, appended to the two autographs of this sonnet, show that M. A. regarded it as a *jeu d'esprit*. '*Per carnovale par lecito far qualche pazzia a chi non va in maschera.*' '*Questo non è fuoco da carnovale, però vel mando di quaresima; e a voi mi racbomando. Vostro Michelagniolo.*'

LXI. Date 1547. No sonnet presents more difficulties than this, in which M. A. has availed himself of a passage in the *Cratylus* of Plato. The divine hammer spoken of in the second couplet is the ideal pattern after which the souls of men are fashioned; and this in the first terzet seems to be identified with Vittoria Colonna. In the second terzet he regards his own soul as imperfect, lacking the final touches which it might have received from hers. See XIV. for a somewhat similar conceit.

LXIV. The image is that of a glowing wood coal smouldering away to embers amid its own ashes.

LXV. Date 1554. Addressed *A messer Giorgio Vasari, amico e pittor singulare*, with this letter: *Messer Giorgio, amico caro, voi direte ben ch' io sie vecchio e pazzo a voler far sonetti; ma perchè molti dicono ch' io son rimbambito, ho voluto far l'uficio mio, ec. A dì 19 di settembre 1554. Vostro Michelagniolo Buonarroti in Roma.*

LXVI., LXVII. These two sonnets were sent to Giorgio Vasari in 1555 (?) with this letter: *Messer Giorgio, io vi mando due sonetti; e benchè sieno cosa sciocca, il fo perchè*

*veggiate dove io tengo i mie' pensieri: e quando arete
ottantuno anni, come ò io, mi crederete. Pregovi gli diate a
messer Giovan Francesco Fattucci, che me ne à chiesti.
Vostro Michelagniolo Buonarroti in Roma.* The first was
also sent to Monsignor Beccadelli, Archbishop of Ragusa,
who replied to it. For his sonnet, see Signor Guasti's
edition, p. 233.

LXVIII. Date 1556. Written in reply to his friend's
invitation that he should pay him a visit at Ragusa. Line
10: this Urbino was M. A.'s old and faithful servant,
Francesco d'Amadore di Casteldurante, who lived with him
twenty-six years, and died at Rome in 1556.

LXIX.-LXXVII. The dates of this series of peniten-
tial sonnets are not known. It is clear that they were
written in old age. It will be remembered that the latest
piece of marble on which Michael Angelo worked, was the
unfinished Pietà now standing behind the choir of the
Duomo at Florence. Many of his latest drawings are
designs for a Crucifixion.

APPENDICES.

I

THE 'Rivista Europea' of June 1875 publishes an article by Signor V. de Tivoli concerning an inedited sonnet of Michael Angelo, which he deciphered from the Autograph, written upon the back of one of the original drawings in the Taylor Gallery at Oxford. This drawing formed part of the Ottley and Lawrence Collection. It represents horses in various attitudes, together with a skirmish between a mounted soldier and a group of men on foot. Signor de Tivoli not only prints the text with all its orthographical confusions, abbreviations, and alterations; but he also adds what he modestly terms a restoration of the sonnet. Of this restoration I have made the subjoined version in rhyme, though I frankly admit that the difficulties of the text, as given in the rough by Signor de Tivoli, seem to me insuperable, and that his readings, though ingenious, cannot in my opinion be accepted as absolutely certain. He himself describes the MS. as a palimpsest, deliberately defaced by Michael Angelo, from which the words originally written have to be recovered in many cases by a process of conjecture. That the style of the restoration is thoroughly Michael Angelesque, will be admitted by all students of Signor Guasti's edition. The only word I felt inclined to question, is *donne* in line 13, where I should have expected *donna*. But I am informed that about this word there is no doubt. The sonnet itself ranks among the less interesting and the least finished compositions of the poet's old age.

Thrice blest was I what time thy piercing dart
    I could withstand and conquer in days past:
    But now my breast with grief is overcast;
    Against my will I weep, and suffer smart.
And if those shafts, aimed with so fierce an art,
    The mark of my frail bosom over-passed,
    Now canst thou take revenge with blows at last
    From those fair eyes which must consume my heart.
O Love, how many a net, how many a snare
    Shuns through long years the bird by fate malign,
    Only at last to die more piteously!
Thus love hath let me run as free as air,
    Ladies, through many a year, to make me pine
    In sad old age, and a worse death to die.

II

The following translations of a madrigal, a quatrain, and
a stanza by Michael Angelo, may be worth insertion here
for the additional light they throw upon some of the pre-
ceding sonnets—especially upon Sonnets I. and II. and
Sonnets LXV.-LXXVII. In my version of the stanza I
have followed Michelangelo the younger's reading.

DIALOGUE OF FLORENCE AND HER EXILES.

Per molti, donna.

'Lady, for joy of lovers numberless
    Thou wast created fair as angels are.
    Sure God hath fallen asleep in heaven afar,
    When one man calls the bliss of many his!
    Give back to streaming eyes
    The daylight of thy face that seems to shun
    Those who must live defrauded of their bliss!'
'Vex not your pure desire with tears and sighs:
    For he who robs you of my light, hath none.
    Dwelling in fear, sin hath no happiness;
    Since amid those who love, their joy is less,
    Whose great desire great plenty still curtails,
    Than theirs who, poor, have hope that never fails.'

APPENDICES.

THE SPEECH OF NIGHT.

Caro m' è 'l sonno.

Sweet is my sleep, but more to be mere stone,
So long as ruin and dishonor reign;
To bear nought, to feel nought, is my great gain;
Then wake me not, speak in an undertone!

LAMENT FOR LIFE WASTED.

Ohimè, ohimè!

Ah me! Ah me! whene'er I think
Of my past years, I find that none
Among those many years, alas, was mine;
False hopes and longings vain have made me pine,
With tears, sighs, passions, fires, upon life's brink.
Of mortal loves I have known every one.
Full well I feel it now; lost and undone,
From truth and goodness banished far away,
I dwindle day by day.
Longer the shade, more short the sunbeams grow;
While I am near to falling, faint and low.

FINIS.